# JEFF KOONS

**ANTHONY d'OFFAY LONDON**

*RIZZOLI*
NEW YORK

# THE
# JEFF KOONS
# HANDBOOK

My family always showed me a lot of love. And art was always a reward system for me. My father was an interior decorator. So I grew up at a very early age learning that the environment can manipulate your emotions and the way that you feel.

I would go into my father's store and one week, one room would be a kitchen, and the adjoining room would be a living room. I would return the next week and the kitchen had become a den for people to watch television and the other room had become a bedroom. I would feel totally different emotions entering that space. I was being manipulated and I liked it.

The first artwork I remember exhibiting was an oil in the manner of Watteau. It was hung in the window of my father's store, Henry J Koons Interiors, in York, Pennsylvania. He started selling my paintings for hundreds of dollars when I was nine years old – horrendous paintings. This gave me a tremendous amount of confidence. It was very sweet of my father. I received a lot of love when I was a child.

The most memorable art and popular culture in my youth were Dalí, the Beatles, my Saturday morning art class, television, and the objects I would see displayed in my father's showroom windows. My life was innocent and beautiful. I took art lessons from the age of seven and all of my teachers have had a large impact on me, in aesthetics and in life.

After moving to New York in 1977, I worked at the Museum of Modern Art selling memberships. I was the most successful salesman in the Museum's history. But I needed to find a way to finance the production of my art so I moved to Wall Street and sold commodities. This enabled me not only to produce my work but to remain independent from the commercial art world system.

I was always an artist. I've been an artist since I was born. Art has always been a way for me to define my own parameters, to externalise myself. I have no perception of Jeff Koons, absolutely not. Your perception of Jeff Koons is probably much more realistic than mine, because to me I am nonexistent.

Jeff Koons 1992

# CONTENTS

AUTOBIOGRAPHY BY JEFF KOONS 5

INTRODUCTION BY ROBERT ROSENBLUM 11

PHRASES AND PHILOSOPHIES
BY JEFF KOONS 29

THE PRE-NEW 41

THE NEW 47

EQUILIBRIUM 53

LUXURY AND DEGRADATION 63

STATUARY 75

KIEPENKERL 85

ART MAGAZINE ADS 89

BANALITY 97

MADE IN HEAVEN 117

PUPPY 143

CATALOGUE RAISONNE 147

EXHIBITION HISTORY AND SELECTED
BIBLIOGRAPHY 165

# NOTES ON JEFF KOONS
## Robert Rosenblum

Although he is not quite in the same media league as Madonna, Donald and Ivana Trump, or his avowed idols, the Beatles and Michael Jackson, Jeff Koons has been doing pretty well for a mere artist. Featured both on the cover and in the pages of countless art periodicals, he has also turned up again and again in practically every glossy magazine or newspaper at hand, from *Time*, *People*, *Newsweek*, *Cosmopolitan*, *Vanity Fair* and *Playboy* to the *New York Post*, the *Orlando Sentinel*, *Le Figaro*, and the *Düsseldorf Express*. Born in 1955 and trained in art schools in Baltimore and Chicago, Koons in 1977 moved to New York, where he launched his professional career at the Museum of Modern Art in a perfect prophecy of his now famous fusion of art, publicity and money. Beginning at the ticket booth, he ended up in the membership department where, at least by his own count, he raked in $3 million a year for his employer, and then went on to hone his financial skills more finely by working as a Wall Street commodities broker. Inevitably, he also immersed himself in the world of advertising, using its visual blitz for, among other things, some direct sources for his own art, which, in his

'Luxury and Degradation' series of 1986, replicated in billboard size seductive, *tête-a-tête* ads for alcoholic bliss (Bacardi rum, Gordon's gin, Hennessy cognac, Frangelico liqueur – pp.68-73). And in the same year he also designed ads to publicize his own gallery exhibitions using come-on photos where he would pose like a starry-eyed, teenage rock star, adored by bikini-clad girls who would help him round up trade for his latest art hits to be seen in New York, Chicago and Cologne (pp.91-95). His wish 'to communicate with as wide an audience as possible' and his belief that the way to do it now is through the media, 'through TV and advertising, through the film and entertainment industries' may sound disarmingly crass, but its combination of dumb innocence and shrewd calculation is clearly, for an artist born in the 1950s and emerging in the climate of 1980s, less affectation than just plain honesty and commonsense for someone pursuing a career in the arts, including those high-minded art critics who are ever eager to expand their own fame and power through the media but who sneer aristocratically at Koons for doing the same thing.

Ever with his eye on the consumer, this paragon of a successful artist, 1980s style, has built up year by year, from 1979 on, what amounts to a Jeff Koons Gift Shoppe. In his inventory of immaculately wrought, gleamingly new objects, usually produced as multiples, the range of consumer temptations is vast. There are such useful items as Spalding basketballs, tea kettles, Hoover Deluxe shampoo polishers, Shelton wet/dry vacuum cleaners, aqualungs, Baccarat crystal sets and travel bars, as well as a broad spectrum of decorative accessories that can adorn nurseries, rumpus rooms, and boudoirs for every taste and budget: Venetian-glass erotica, stainless-steel trolls and flower arrangements, gilded rococo mirrors, wooden Yorkshire terriers, sculptured icons of veneration such as superstars Michael Jackson, Bob Hope and the artist himself, and for the more conventionally pious, even a polychrome porcelain St. John the Baptist worthy of a Neapolitan souvenir shop. Moreover, by the 1990s, when Koons's liaison with another media star, Ilona Staller, better known as 'La Cicciolina', had been sanctioned by the proprieties of old-fashioned romantic love and marriage, even the couple's most intimate indoor and outdoor sexual raptures could be translated into collectibles in both two and three dimensions, quasi-religious glimpses of an ecstatic, celestial joy that has barely been witnessed since the days when Counter-Reformation artists proselytized the church with a sensuous theatre of transported bodies and souls.

With over a decade's full-power barrage of art,

glamour, fame, bliss and shopping, it is no wonder that the Koons phenomenon has provided grist for every mill. Students of 1980s consumerism can have a field day with his styles of salesmanship, the baroque translation of Barbara Kruger's tough, terse and hard-edged visual slogan: I SHOP THERE-FORE I AM. Autograph hounds haunting art-world personality cults are happy to identify him as the legitimate heir to Warhol and Dalí with his mix of self-display and instant global media coverage. Observers of the once out-of-bounds territory of democratic taste can now add him to the cultural company of those sophisticated, jet-setting archi-tects – Michael Graves, Robert Stern, Arata Isozaki, Frank Gehry – who are happy to put their populist tents down in the Disney Empire. Porno stars like Annie Sprinkle can take on another side of Koons by writing a nuts-and-bolts review of his X-rated exhibition, 'Made in Heaven', speaking as one hard-core performer to another (see *Arts*, March 1992). And even the duller domain of art-world lawyers can now claim Koons as a major player, after he became the victim of a court ruling that he had violated copyright by appropriating, for one of his polychrome wooden sculptures, a cornball commercial photograph of a couple hold-ing eight German shepherd puppies, an outrageous verdict that could have frightening consequences for countless artists, from Van Gogh and Picasso to Lichtenstein and Mike Bidlo.

All these unbalancing angles of vision, naturally, create endless fodder for every form of juicy gossip, snobbish contempt, dropped-jaw bewilderment, or even cool sociological analysis. Koons deserves all of this and more; yet the aura of publicity around him often deflects attention from the bottom-line fact that he is first of all an artist, and one whose work belongs to the history of art, looking backwards, forwards and sideways in the visual company of not only his contemporaries but of older generations.

In terms of first-person experience, I still recall the shock of my initial confrontation with Koons's lovingly hideous and accurate reconstructions of the lowest levels of three-dimensional kitsch, from porcelain Pink Panthers and Popples to painted wooden bears and angels. We all, of course, have been seeing this kind of stuff for years in every shopping centre and tourist trap, but never before have we been forced, as one is in a gallery setting, to look head on and up close at its mind-boggling ugliness and deliriously vapid expressions. The bells that finally rang, at least for me, chimed all the way back to 1962, when I first saw Lichtenstein's earliest Pop paintings at Leo Castelli's and stared with disbelief at the colossal gall of an artist who would pollute the space of art with such contemptibly lowbrow images. But then, having regained a bit of balance, I stared again with a wide-eyed awe and fascination before the both familiar and somehow never-before seen visual and emotional facts of that flood of cheap commercial and comic-strip illustrations that gluts us in the real world but that had been censored out of an art world where educated taste was thought to reign. Just as Lichtenstein, in the early 1960s, compelled us to peer in amazement, like modern Gullivers, at this alarmingly grotesque, but ubiquitous visual environment in which we were all living, like it or not, so too did Koons, two decades later, proclaim a new segment of popular bad taste as his own, rubbing our eyes in it and forcing us to look, really look, at this bizarre species of art that covers our planet and that pleases millions.

If it is true that one of the exalting effects of art is to make us see, often for the first time, the commonplace realities that surround us, by transforming and relocating them in a more purified, contemplative terrain, then Koons's success is total. Over and over again, what might have been a boring or trashy spectacle in this or that corner of a department store, mail-order catalogue or toy shop, has magically been reincarnated as art. At the shopping mall or airport store, we can now pause before, say, a particularly repulsive cuckoo clock, complete with smiling peasants in lederhosen, artificial geraniums and an airborne flurry of chirping, Disneyesque birds, and tip our hats towards the artist who made it suddenly visible, wrenching it into the surprising context of prolonged scrutiny in the loftier territory of art seen in museums and galleries. 'This', we think, 'would make a perfect Jeff Koons', just as a line-up of Campbell's soup cans or a city wall covered with graffiti is now quickly converted into this or that modern artist. Art has a miraculous way of exorcising and healing what used to be eyesores.

In this, Koons often resurrects, as do many artists of his generation, the spirit of 1960s Pop, which enthusiastically embraced the visual pollutions of the crass world out there as if to say, 'If you can't lick it, join it.' Of course by the 1980s this battle had already been won, and Koons and his contemporaries, unlike Warhol and his, no longer had to fight their way through the elitist assumptions of abstract art and could stand comfortably in the triumphs of a now venerable tradition of wallowing in, rather than shielding themselves from, the facts of daily life in a civilization bombarded by commercial come-ons. So it is, for example, that Koons's five-foot wide clones of liquor ads update in a less rebellious and ironic way Rosenquist's innovative recreations, in the 1960s, of the overscaled, textureless consumer bait dangled on American billboards, much as Koons's early selection of products that would join the hygienic, hi-tech war on dirt and wear – vacuum cleaners, electric brooms, floor polishers – had its ancestor in Lichtenstein's more low-budget encyclopedia of products such as kitchen sponges, spray cleaners, step-on garbage cans.

Koons's inventory of ads and goods from the 1980s, which updated the consumer catalogues of Pop Art, was shared, in fact, by many of his contemporaries. His choice of sexy liquor ads, for example, parallels Richard Prince's rephotographing of the macho cowboys who would addict us to Marlboro cigarettes. Similarly, his infatuation with the pristine, commercial arrangement of brand-new, dust-free factory products, often in airtight plastic vitrines and arranged as multiples, has its counterpart in the department-store shelf displays of Haim Steinbach, just as his attraction to the visual complexities of technological gear overlaps Ashley Bickerton's science-fictional explorations of the spotless intricacies of equipment so strange that it looks ready for use on the moon or the bottom of the sea.

Often too, Koons's isolation of the odd artifacts of our culture, whether utilitarian, playful, commemorative, or aesthetic, harks back to many earlier artists' efforts to embalm objects we take for granted, as if they were to be treasured as rare archaeological finds from our century, the stuff of time capsules. Duchamp, father of so many things, may have set this 20th-century form of taxidermy into motion by transforming, in a deceptively direct way, anything from a urinal to a bicycle wheel into a mysterious witness of our civilization; and Johns, closer in spirit to the world into which Koons was born, continued to make these modern relics by petrifying forever, in bronze or sculp-metal, the now useless fossil remains of flashlights, toothbrushes, light-bulbs, and ale cans. Koons's more glitzy, 1980s nouveau-riche approach involves a comparable form of flash-freezing for posterity. A basketball is preserved like a precious object in a museum vitrine, afloat forever in an aquarium on a pedestal (p.59). An inflatable dinghy with its oars is immobilized in a bronze cast. A child's dime-store toy such as a throwaway blow-up vinyl bunny with carrot in hand and jerky smile, first used in its original form in 1979, is seven years later metamorphosed for eternity in one of Koons's favourite media, stainless steel, creating a bizarrely indestructible idol like something from an unidentified cult (p.83). And the reflective, unperishable armour of this archetypal 20th-century synthetic metal (in Koons's words, 'the symbol of the proletariat, a poor man's luxury') is also used to stop in its tracks both past and present time, whether in a 3-D caricature of comedian Bob Hope, with grotesquely swollen head, or in a baroque bust of a bewigged absolute monarch, à la Louis XIV (p.77), works that might evoke, beneath their ever-glistening surfaces, anything from 17th-century hand-carved marble craftsmanship fit for a King to an infinity of factory-made reproductions in a souvenir shop. Koons's Hall of Fame demonstrates his faith that 'statuary presents a panoramic view of society; on the one hand there is Louis XIV and on the other hand there is Bob Hope.' Leveling different centuries and different kinds of glory to a populist, Disney World perspective, he makes portrait busts for modern consumers interested in a serious purchase for home display that, like an Oscar or an athletic trophy, will also become a precious heirloom.

In many of the earlier works from 1979 to 1986 Koons often seemed to offer belated, though original, variations on the repetitive, minimalist geometries of the 1960s and 70s (his Spalding basketballs symmetrically suspended in their tanks are odd deductions from the abstract tradition of juggling pure spheres and cubes) and even the sleek ovoid shapes of his stainless-steel bunny have been located under the shadow of Brancusi's organic distillations. But he also began to move away from these modernist austerities into a far more startlingly unfamiliar language of baroque style, especially as seen in its most debased 20th-century progeny. Koons, in fact, explored not only the folkloric mode found in kitsch souvenirs in which the painstakingly realist description of cherubs, poodles, or cuddly pigs offers the last vulgar gasps of the stone- and wood-carver's veristic handicraft that had contributed to the glories of baroque and rococo sculpture, but also the grander, more palatial baroque heritage familiar to the world of Liberace and Mafia furniture emporia, and often encountered in late 19th-century extravaganzas such as Ludwig II's Bavarian castles Herrenchiemsee (neo-Versailles) and Linderhof (neo-Louis XV). And in one unforgettable *tour-de-force*, Koons even managed to wed the genuine and the neo. In the summer of 1992, as part of an exhibition of contemporary art held at Schloss Arolsen, less than an hour from Kassel's Documenta 9, he was able to join forces with the early 18th-century castle, which became the theatrical setting for a Koons extravaganza, a colossus of kitsch in the form of a puppy, almost 40-feet high, who sits in the courtyard like the most adorable of guard dogs (p.145). Made of thousands of flowering plants, from petunias and geraniums to begonias and chrysanthemums, this giant topiary toy telescopes the old and the new baroque, mixing memories of the kind of fantastic garden follies which were meant to dazzle the absolute monarchs who could afford them with the most deliriously deviant branches off that old tree, whether the flower floats at the annual Rose Bowl pageants or the animal-shaped hedges that greet visitors to Orlando's Disney World.

Given the fact that the baroque and rococo styles have been, for the better part of this century, uncomfortably at odds with good taste and with the look of modern art and design, Koons's espousal of this historical vocabulary of decorative excess, often demoted in our time to things like vintage carousels and early movie theatres, was a startling transgression, outside even the most relaxed modernist canons. His own aphorisms declare his admiration for the church's use of baroque and rococo style to give a false sense of luxury and economic security in order to concentrate on more spiritual experiences, a goal he at times claims to pursue. Initially, Koons's productions in this historic language were objects of modest ornamental ambition, such as a gilded rococo mirror or a stainless-steel version of a porcelain 18th-century couple in a Cinderella coach, but soon they soared to a would-be spiritual peak on the crest of the oceanic waves of love that swept him and La Cicciolina away, and bore out to an infamous degree his succinct statement, 'My art and my life are totally one'. Koons was to produce the greatest love story of all time, his own.

In what quickly was to become his most startling and publicity-hungry works, an on-going series offered under the cinematic title, 'Made in Heaven', he and La Cicciolina carried the bliss of perfect love, marriage, and sex to such celestial climes that we would hardly be surprised to find a Jesuit saint ascending with them to a joyful, cloud-borne eternity. Indeed, Koons's overtly outrageous boast that his work 'functions very much on the level of the church' may not be so off the mark. So lofty were his spiritual ambitions for this paean to erotic fulfillment that in one of the over-life-size photographs (p.122), he even paraphrased the posture of Michelangelo's nude Adam, joining himself to an almost-nude Eve (who wears a few modern accessories such as silver spike-heel shoes and an open bra) and setting this double allegorical portrait against a cosmic turmoil that provides an appropriately extraterrestrial backdrop for the primal scene. 'We are the contemporary Adam and Eve' is, in fact, just what he said when commenting about the 1989 billboard (p.119) that advertised his forthcoming, but eventually scrapped movie,

'Made in Heaven'. And if Biblical and old-master archetypes lurk behind this conception, so, of course, does the more up-to-date mythology of the movies. Their eternal embraces recall, among other unforgettable shots in our collective image banks, Deborah Kerr and Burt Lancaster's 'From Here to Eternity' clinch amidst the passionate roar of surf against sand. Koons's constant advice – 'to embrace your past' – is almost literally heeded in this epic fusion of memories both lofty and popular, ancient and modern.

These images of transcendental sensuality were first presented at the 1990 Venice Biennale, where, seen in the company of so many other artists' displays, their candid couplings in both mural-sized colour photographs and waxworks-like statues produced the clandestine peep-show mood that decades ago made it possible only for gentlemen tourists, but not ladies, to see behind locked museum doors the 'dirty' Roman art culled from Pompeii and Herculaneum. Rapidly, the sexual pressures of these embraces pushed the images into X-rated territory, so that the 1991 Christmas show at New York's Sonnabend Gallery was to be kept out of the sight of unaccompanied minors and may even have traumatized those relatively few innocent SoHo art lovers who stumbled upon the show by accident, without having heard through the media that pornography and contemporary art had been scandalously wedded for a month.

Among other amazing things about this group of images, which replaced the earlier, relatively discreet concealment of pudenda with gynecologically bald close-ups of genital unions worthy of the Kamasutra, was that, of all unlikely things, art totally vanquished, or rather absorbed, sex. Instead of a porno show, the effect was like that of Japanese erotic prints, where the degree of stylization is so exaggerated that the sexual acrobatics as such are quickly submerged in an all-engulfing artifice. Here, the cinemascopic baroque universe that would fuse heaven and earth, flesh and spirit exorcised the lurid parts, which, at least as far as La Cicciolina was concerned, were so thoroughly depilated, cherubically pink, and spotlessly clean, that they almost would have been at home in an exhibition of 19th-century academic nudes, at once wanton and idealized, by the likes of Bouguereau or Cabanel. And in 'Made in Heaven' the heat of the torrid images was also cooled and sweetened by the inclusion, as in a wrap-around installation, of other kinds of Koonsiana, from soulfully chaste neo-baroque marble busts of the artist and his blessed wife to the more familiar repertory of dogs, birds, cats and flowers; all works that invoked such wholesome, Disney World family values that their very presence at this exhibition provided a fortress against any thoughts of obscenity. After all, back in 1988, Koons had already displayed an almost Victorian faith in the virtues of innocence by creating a childhood version of Adam and Eve on a flower-strewn heart: two stark naked children who sweetly embrace in a world unpolluted by Freud (p.101). Could the creator of this old-fashioned banality be identified as your everyday pornographer? If we may take the artist at his word, it was not pornography at all that interested him, but love, reunion and spiritual matters, exalted emotions whose corny but time-honoured rhetoric quickly eclipsed the X-rated components of 'Made in Heaven'. Moreover, by showing his kitschy flower arrangements, with exposed pistil and stamen, in the midst of a display of usually secret human orifices and projections, Koons was eager to underline the biological equation between the world of botany and our own private parts.

'Made in Heaven' also became a revelation in terms of testing the limits of late 20th-century censorship. Until something is shown, no-one can guess what new breach of propriety is permissible in a public art space. It was only in the 1980s that X-rated Picassos, featuring delirious copulations and every kind of indecent exposure, could be included comfortably in museum retrospectives and tour the world without protest; and it was in 1988 that the Brooklyn Museum offered in its Courbet exhibition the landmark debut of the artist's notorious *Origin of the World*, a formerly secret painting for a private patron that offered a head-on disclosure of what lay between a woman's thighs. Seen within the context of artists of great stature who had many other things to offer besides genitals at rest or in action, these works were absorbed with little or no fuss into the art-world repertory.

Looked at from this vantage point, Koons's art also belongs to the collective history of the public acceptance, at least in the domain of art, of overt sex. It is telling that, only months after Koons's New York show of winter 1991, Cindy Sherman also unveiled in SoHo a series of equally theatrical photographs of grotesquely prosthetic male and female sexual parts, devouring each other in infantile, nightmarish scenes that seem to have been invented in Freud's id. This series provided almost the perfect counterpart to Koons's 'Made in Heaven', and might even have been aptly titled 'Made in Hell'. Both artists flagrantly violated earlier standards of sexual decorum in public, mural-scaled art and both did so by translating their erotic imaginations into a language of total artifice, fraught with art-historical echoes. If Koons reincarnated Bernini's Santa Teresa, Sherman took us on a contemporary trip to Bosch's hell.

Once again, Koons, who may seem to be living in a distant media world surrounded by the same news reporters and cameramen who go after Michael Jackson, is also living right in the middle of the world of less flashy fellow artists. No matter where we look, he figures large. If we consider how the old-fashioned classifications of painter, sculptor, photographer have become anachronisms for many younger artists who belong to all or none of these categories, then Koons is a key player. If we think about the strange new race of three-dimensional humanoids and mannequins spawned in the last few decades by artists as different as Duane Hanson and Charles Ray, or about the way in which, as with Mike Kelley, the real toys and souvenirs of an American childhood have become central to a new repertory of artists' themes, he plays a no less central role. And if we think about that breed of artists whose life and art appear inseparable, such as Joseph Beuys, Gilbert & George, McDermott & McGough, then Koons is also a major figure. Self-promoting as he may sound when he claims that 'Jeff Koons is a person who is trying to lead art into the 21st century', he also happens to be right.

# PHRASES AND PHILOSOPHIES BY JEFF KOONS

Jeff Koons is a victim, and I hope that everyone is a victim. One must be victimized in order to absorb one's culture and to participate. If people can accept that position they will be able to listen closely to life. Life will be a close-up.

My work has no aesthetic values, other than the aesthetics of communication.

I believe that taste is really unimportant.

Art can, and should, be used to stimulate social mobility. I envisage the formation of a total society where every citizen will be of blue blood. In such a society the individual will exist in a state of entropy, or rest, and will inhabit an environment decorated with object art that is beyond critical dialogue.

Through my work, I tell people to embrace their past, to embrace who they are. By doing so, they will have a foundation to work from. I have embraced my past and I appreciate the beauty in it.

Salesmen are today's great communicators. They are out there pushing cars, real estate, advertising. That is where the real morality is played out in society today.

I communicate to people that you do not have to be intelligent in life. It's enough to be clever.

A viewer might at first see irony in my work, but I see none at all. Irony causes too much critical contemplation.

I'm for the return of the objective, and for the artist to regain the responsibility for manipulation and seduction: for art to have as much political impact as the entertainment industry, the film, the pop music and the advertising industries.

The art world can be absolutely anything. The only

thing the art world does need is people to lead it beyond its parameters.

I am trying to capture the individual's desire in the object, and to fix his or her aspirations in the surface, in a condition of immortality.

Debasement is what gives the bourgeois freedom.

I believe artists must exploit themselves, and they must also take the responsibility to exploit their viewers.

My work embraces, it communicates. That's what is threatening to people, because it is looking for a direct response; it's looking to form a dialogue.

I believe the way to enter the eternal is through the biological.

The door to the eternal is open to everyone through generosity. Generosity makes fear disappear, and when fear is gone, guilt and shame follow: one is liberated.

I am completely adaptable. I will adapt to any situation in order to communicate.

Pornography is alienation.
My work has absolutely no
vocabulary in alienation. It's
about using sexuality as a tool
to communicate.

I have my finger on the Eternal.

If art is not directed toward the
social, it becomes purely self-
indulgent, like sex without
love. But if art is functioning in
the social sphere and helping
to define social order, it's
working purely as a tool of
philosophy, enhancing the
quality of individual life and
re-directing social and political
attitudes. Art can define an
individual's aspirations and
goals just as other systems –

economics, for instance – are defining them now. Art can define ultimate states of being in a more responsible way than economics because art is concerned with philosophy as well as with the marketplace.

Abstraction and luxury are the guard dogs of the upper class.

I never try to degrade my ideas to make them more accessible. The vocabulary always tries to achieve mobility, to bring the aristocracy down and the lower classes up.

At one time, artists had only to whisper into the ear of the King or Pope to have political effect. Now, they must whisper into the ears of millions of people.

The most perverse thing for me is to know one's limitations and still to have the desire to lead. And when you lead you know you have chosen a dead end because there are so many options and so many directions to take people. This is the perversion that I enjoy most.

In the art world I have always found everyone very weak. The art world really has been up for grabs. Anybody who has enough desire to lead, it's there for them to do. Because

no one else wants it.
Absolutely not.

If I've reached the bourgeois
class, anybody can.

Morality has always played a
very important part in my work.
Many times I will go to the
depths of hypocrisy and
resurface without making any
direct moral judgement. By
some I am viewed as a sinner
but I am really a saint. God has
always been on my side.
Anyone with enough distance
will be able to find my positive
moral position.

Contradiction is a powerful
tool. You cannot liberate

everyone. The contradictions in my personality run deep. In part, I am a sham, a con man. But I also have a sense of integrity that I hope comes through in my work.

Jeff Koons

# THE PRE-NEW

1979

In the 'Pre-New' I was manipulating objects. I was not maintaining the objects' integrity. I would glue a teapot to plastic tubes or put a bolt through the back of a coffee percolator. What was important in this work is that it liberated me from my own subjective sexuality. I was taking my work into the realm of the objective. I was distancing myself from my own sexuality.

Teapot 1979

Hoover Celebrity III is the first vacuum cleaner piece. I chose the vacuum cleaner because of its anthropomorphic qualities. It is a breathing machine. It also displays both male and female sexuality. It has orifices and phallic attachments. I have always tried to create work which does not alienate any part of my audience.

Hoover Celebrity III 1980

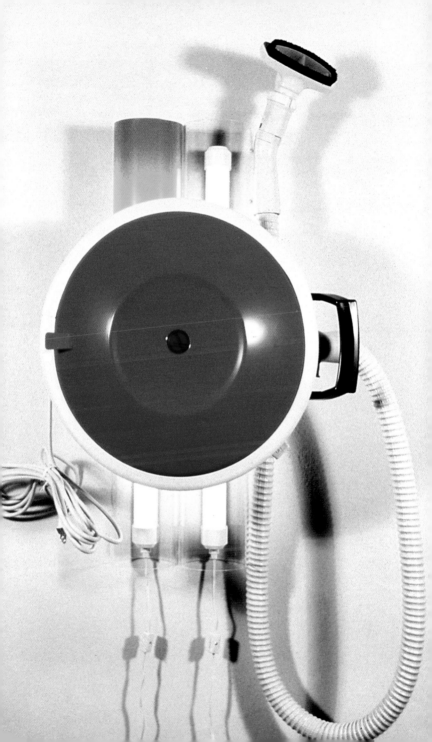

# THE NEW

1980-86

In the body of work I called 'The New', I was interested in a psychological state tied to newness and immortality: the gestalt came directly from viewing an inanimate object – a vacuum cleaner – that was in a position to be immortal.

New Hoover Convertibles, New Shelton Wet/Dry Doubledecker 1981-86

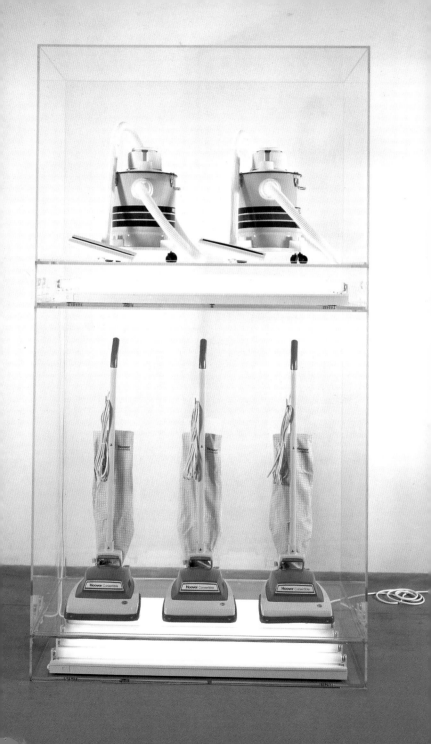

I have always used cleanliness and a form of order to maintain for the viewer a belief in the essence of the eternal, so that the viewer does not feel threatened economically. When under economic pressure you start to see disintegration around you. Things do not remain orderly. So I have always placed order in my work not out of a respect for minimalism, but to give the viewer a sense of economic security.

New Hoover Deluxe Shampoo
Polishers 1981-86

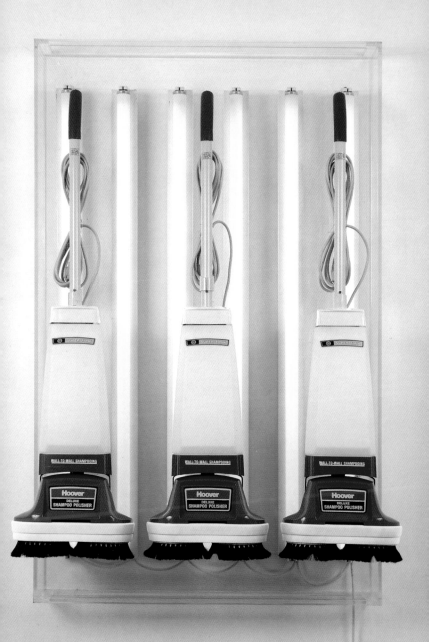

# EQUILIBRIUM

1985

Where I see art going, its exchange value, its economic substructure, will be removed: it will function solely as a means of support and security. From this point of view, my work has strong biological implications: the encasement of the vacuum cleaners with the ideas of removal and protection, and the equilibrium tanks with water suspending basketballs – these are all very womblike.

One Ball Total Equilibrium Tank 1985

I want to have an impact
in people's lives. I want to
communicate to as wide a
mass as possible. And the
way to communicate with the
public right now is through TV
and advertising. The art world
is not effective right now.

Moses 1985

Aqualung is a tool for equilibrium; if someone had enough courage and really wanted to go for it, they would put the Aqualung on their back and it would take them under.

Aqualung 1985

The tanks are ultimate states of being and for me they are also the beginning of artifical intelligence. Due to vibration, the basketballs move. This changes the pattern of information communicated between them. This is the beginning of independent thought patterns.

Three Ball 50/50 Tank 1985

# LUXURY AND DEGRADATION

1986

In 'Luxury and Degradation' the objects are given an artificial luxury, an artificial value, which transforms them completely, changing their function, and, to a certain extent, decriticalizing them. My surface is very much a false front for an underlying degradation.

Fisherman Golfer 1986

Jim Beam – J.B. Turner Train 1986

"I

I Could Go for Something Gordon's 1986

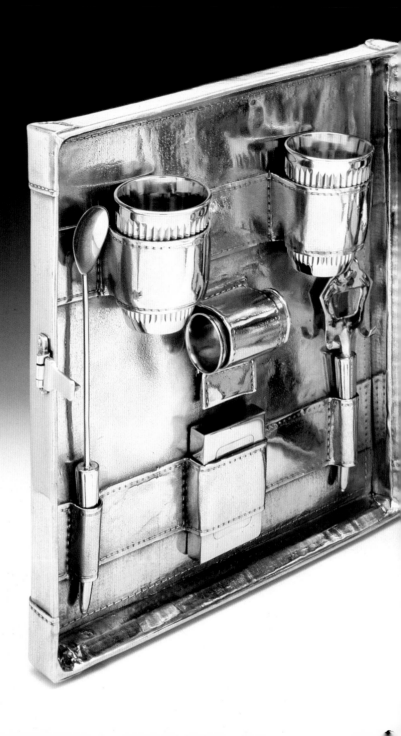

Travel Bar 1986

In the liquor advertisements, the purpose was not so much to direct the viewer as to define social class structure. For example, the Frangelico ads define a $45,000 and up income, and are more concerned with being lost in one's own thought patterns. The public is being deceived in these advertisements on different levels of thought, because they are educated in abstraction and luxury on different levels of income.

Stay in Tonight 1986

Stay in tonight.

# STATUARY

1986

'Statuary' presents a panoramic view of society: on one side there is Louis XIV and on the other side there is Bob Hope. If you put art in the hands of the monarch it will reflect his ego and eventually become decorative. If you put art in the hands of the masses, it will reflect mass ego and eventually become decorative. If you put art in the hands of Jeff Koons it will reflect my ego and eventually become decorative.

Louis XIV 1986

My art has always used sex as a direct communication line to the viewer. The surface of my stainless steel pieces is pure sex and gives an object both a masculine and a feminine side: the weight of the steel engages with the femininity of the reflective surface.

Doctor's Delight 1986

Flowers 1986

I'm making some of the greatest art being made now. It'll take the art world ten years to get around to it. In this century there was Picasso and Duchamp. Now I'm taking us out of the twentieth century.

Rabbit 1986

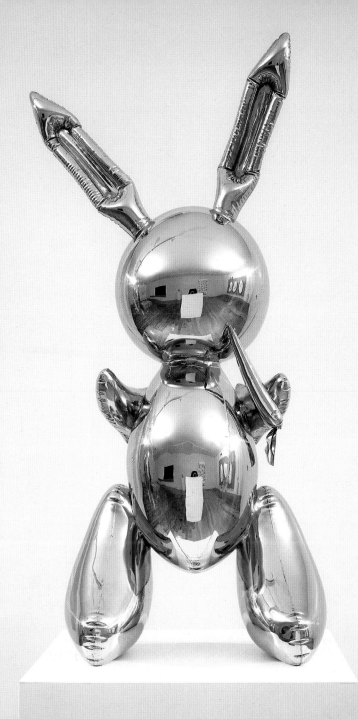

KIEPENKERL

1986

Kiepenkerl was my 'Humpty Dumpty'. Everything was a total fiasco. I decided to give the piece radical plastic surgery, somehow to get it together again so I could display it. Through this radical work on it, through having craftsmen work and bend and not maintain the integrity of the original model, I was liberated to go on to 'Banality' and to use the public as a ready-made instead of any object.

Kiepenkerl 1986

ART MAGAZINE ADS

1988-89

I was there with two pigs – a big one and a little one – so it was like breeding banality. I wanted to debase myself and call myself a pig before the viewer had a chance to, so that they could only think more of me.

# J E F F   K O O N S

SONNABEND • NEW YORK   MAX HETZLER • KÖLN   DONALD YOUNG • CHICAGO

The Artforum ad shows me
in front of a blackboard
indoctrinating very young
children – kindergarteners and
first-graders – children really
too vulnerable for such an
indoctrination into my art.
I really wanted to direct that
sense of their vulnerability to
the Artforum readership, the
people who hate me, to make
them just grit their teeth and
hate me even more because I
was taking away their future.
I was getting at their future,
the youth of tomorrow.

J E F F  K O O N S
EXPLOIT THE MASSES
BANALITY
SONNABEND • NEW YORK  MAX HETZLER • KÖLN  DONALD YOUNG • CHICAGO

JEFF KOONS

SONNABEND · NEW YORK · MAX HETZLER · KÖLN · DONALD YOUNG · CHICAGO

Arts 1988-89

JEFF KOONS

PHOTO: GREG GORMAN

SONNABEND · NEW YORK · MAX HETZLER · KÖLN · DONALD YOUNG · CHICAGO

Art in America 1988-89

# BANALITY

1988

Everybody grew up surrounded by this material. I try not to use it in any cynical manner. I use it to penetrate mass consciousness – to communicate to people.

In the porcelain pieces I wanted to be able to show the sexuality of the material. Porcelain is a material which was created in the service of the monarch and made in the King's oven. Of course, over the centuries it has become totally democratized but still the material always wants to return to the service of the monarch. There is this uplifting quality about it, this feeling of one's social standing being increased just by being around the material.

Naked 1988

Ushering in Banality 1988

Pink Panther is about masturbation. I don't know what she would be doing with the Pink Panther other than taking it home to masturbate with.

I use the Baroque to show the public that we are in the realm of the spiritual, the eternal. The church uses the Baroque to manipulate and seduce, but in return it does give the public a spiritual experience. My work deals in the vocabulary of the Baroque.

St. John the Baptist 1988

Michael Jackson and Bubbles 1988

When you go to church and you see the gold and the Rococo, it's there, they say, for the glory of God. But I believe that it's there just to soothe the masses for the moment; to make them feel economically secure; to let something else – a spiritual experience, a manipulation – come into their lives.

Christ and the Lamb 1988

I've tried to make work that any viewer, no matter where they came from, would have to respond to, would have to say that on some level 'Yes, I like it.' If they couldn't do that, it would only be because they had been told they were not supposed to like it. Eventually they will be able to strip all that down and say 'You know, it's silly, but I like that piece. It's great.'

Stacked 1988

I've made what the Beatles would have made if they had made sculpture. Nobody ever said that the Beatles' music was not on a high level, but it appealed to a mass audience. That's what I want to do.

Bear and Policeman 1988

MADE IN HEAVEN

1989-92

MADE
IN
HEAVEN

PHOTO: RICCARDO SCHICCHI

Made in Heaven 1989

My art and my life are totally one. I have everything at my disposal and I'm doing what I want to do. I have my platform, I have the attention, and my voice can be heard. This is the time for Jeff Koons.

Self-Portrait 1991

Jeff in the Position of Adam 1990

Yorkshire Terriers 1991

In the Large Vase of Flowers there are 140 flowers. They are very sexual and fertile, and at the same time they are 140 assholes.

Cherubs 1991

I went through moral conflict. I could not sleep for a long time in the preparation of my new work. I had to go to the depths of my own sexuality, my own morality, to be able to remove fear, guilt and shame from myself. All of this has been removed for the viewer. So when the viewer sees it, they are in the realm of the Sacred Heart of Jesus.

Wolfman 1991

Violet Ice (Kama Sutra) 1991

Poodle 1991

Manet 1991

Embrace your past.

Wall Relief with Bird 1991

Ilona and I were born for each other. She's a media woman. I'm a media man. We are the contemporary Adam and Eve.

I believe totally that I'm in the realm of the spiritual, now, with Ilona. Through our union, we're aligned once again with nature. I mean we've become God. That's the bottom line – we've become God.

Bourgeois Bust – Jeff and Ilona 1991

PUPPY

1992

Puppy communicates love, warmth and happiness to everyone. I created a contemporary Sacred Heart of Jesus.

# CATALOGUE RAISONNE

Works of 1979 to 1992, arranged
chronologically by exhibition and
alphabetically by title. Page
numbers are given for works
illustrated.

## INFLATABLES
(Selected)

*Inflatable Flowers
(Short Pink, Tall Yellow)*
1979
Plastic, mirrors, Plexiglas
16 × 25 × 18 ins

*Inflatable Flower and Bunny
(Tall Yellow and Pink Bunny)*
1979
Plastic, mirrors, Plexiglas
32 × 25 × 18 ins

*Inflatable Flowers
(Tall Yellow, Tall Orange)*
1979
Plastic, mirrors
16 × 25 × 18 ins

*Inflatable Flowers
(Short Pink, Tall Purple)*
1979
Plastic, mirrors, Plexiglas
16 × 25 × 18 ins

## THE PRE-NEW
(Selected)

*Hoover Celebrity III*
1980
Vacuum cleaner, acrylic,
fluorescent lights
38 × 20 × 11 ins
(illustrated p.45)

*Nelson Automatic Cooker/
Deep Fryer*
1979
Appliance, acrylic, fluorescent
lights
24 × 32 × 16 ins

*Teapot*
1979
Teapot, acrylic, fluorescent lights
27 × 9 × 12 ins
(illustrated p.43)

*Telephone*
1979
Telephone, mirror, Plexiglas
16 × 12 × 2$^1/_2$ ins

*Toaster*
1979
Toaster, acrylic, fluorescent lights
27 × 9 × 13 ins

## THE NEW

*New 100's Merit Ultra-Lights*
1981
Colour Duratran, lightbox
42 × 63 × 8 ins

*New Double Shelton Wet/Dry*
1980
Two vacuum cleaners, Plexiglas,
fluorescent lights
54 × 43 × 28 ins

*New Hoover Celebrity III's*
1980
Two vacuum cleaners, Plexiglas,
fluorescent lights
56 × 30 × 12$^1$/$_2$ ins

*New Hoover Celebrity IV &
Quik-Broom*
1980
Two vacuum cleaners, Plexiglas,
fluorescent lights
56 × 27 × 19$^1$/$_4$ ins

*New Hoover Celebrity IV, New
Hoover Convertible, New Shelton
Wet/Dry 5-Gallon, New Shelton
Wet/Dry 10-Gallon Doubledecker*
1981-1986
Four vacuum cleaners, Plexiglas,
fluorescent lights
99 × 53$^1$/$_2$ × 28 ins

*New Hoover Celebrity QS*
1980-1986
Vacuum cleaner, acrylic,
fluorescent lights
54 × 27 × 19 ins

*New Hoover Convertible*
1980
Vacuum cleaner, Plexiglas,
fluorescent lights
56 × 22$^1$/$_2$ × 22$^1$/$_2$ ins

*New Hoover Convertible, New
Shelton Wet/Dry 5-Gallon, New
Shelton Wet/Dry 5-Gallon
Displaced Doubledecker*
1981-1987
Three vacuum cleaners, Plexiglas,
fluorescent lights
99 × 54 × 28 ins

*New Hoover Convertible, New
Shelton Wet/Dry 10-Gallon
Doubledecker*
1981
Two vacuum cleaners, Plexiglas,
fluorescent lights
99 × 28 × 28 ins

*New Hoover Convertibles*
1984
Two vacuum cleaners, Plexiglas,
fluorescent lights
58 × 41 × 28 ins

*New Hoover Convertibles, Green,
Blue, New Hoover Convertibles,
Green, Blue, Doubledecker*
1981-1987
Four vacuum cleaners, Plexiglas,
fluorescent lights
116 × 41 × 28 ins

*New Hoover Convertibles Green,
Green, Red, New Hoover Deluxe
Shampoo Polishers, New Shelton
Wet/Dry 5-Gallon Displaced
Tripledecker*
1981-1987
Five vacuum cleaners, two
shampoo polishers, Plexiglas,
fluorescent lights
123 × 54 × 28 ins

*New Hoover Convertibles, Green,*
*Red, Brown, New Hoover Deluxe*
*Shampoo Polishers, Yellow,*
*Brown Doubledecker*
1981-1986
Three vacuum cleaners, two
shampoo polishers, Plexiglas,
fluorescent lights
83 × 54 × 28 ins

*New Hoover Convertibles, Green,*
*Red, Brown, New Shelton*
*Wet/Dry 10-Gallon Displaced*
*Doubledecker*
1981-1987
Four vacuum cleaners, Plexiglas,
fluorescent lights
99 × 54 × 28 ins

*New Hoover Convertibles, New*
*Shelton Wet/Dry Doubledecker*
1981-1986
Three vacuum cleaners, Plexiglas,
fluorescent lights
99 × 41 × 28 ins
(illustrated p 51)

*New Hoover Convertibles, New*
*Shelton Wet/Dry 5-Gallon*
*Displaced Doubledecker*
1981-1987
Three vacuum cleaners, Plexiglas,
fluorescent lights
99 × 41 × 28 ins

*New Hoover Convertibles, New*
*Shelton Wet/Drys 5-Gallon*
*Doubledecker*
1981-1986
Four vacuum cleaners, Plexiglas,
fluorescent lights
99 × 54 × 28 ins

*New Hoover Convertibles, New*
*Shelton Wet/Drys 5-Gallon*
*Doubledecker*
1981-1987
Five vacuum cleaners, Plexiglas,
fluorescent lights
99 × 54 × 28 ins

*New Hoover Deluxe Rug*
*Shampooer*
1979
Rug shampooer, Plexiglas,
fluorescent lights
53 × 10 × 13 ins

*New Hoover Deluxe Shampoo*
*Polisher*
1980-1986
Shampoo polisher, Plexiglas,
fluorescent lights
56 × 36 × 15 ins

*New Hoover Deluxe Shampoo*
*Polishers*
1980
Two shampoo polishers, Plexiglas,
fluorescent lights
56 × 22 × 14 ins

*New Hoover Deluxe Shampoo
Polishers*
1980-1986
Three shampoo polishers,
Plexiglas, fluorescent lights
56 × 36 × 15 ins
(illustrated p.49)

*New Hoover Deluxe Shampoo
Polishers, New Hoover Quik-
Broom, New Shelton Wet/Drys
Tripledecker*
1981-1987
Three shampoo polishers, three
vacuum cleaners, Plexiglas,
fluorescent lights
91 × 54 × 28 ins

*New Hoover Deluxe Shampoo
Polishers, New Shelton Wet/Dry
5-Gallon Displaced Quadradecker*
1981-1987
Vacuum cleaner, six shampoo
polishers, Plexiglas, fluorescent
lights
116 × 54 × 28 ins

*New Hoover Deluxe Shampoo
Polishers, New Shelton Wet/Dry
10 Gallon Displaced Tripledecker*
1981-1987
Four shampoo polishers, vacuum
cleaner, Plexiglas, fluorescent
lights
91 × 54 × 28 ins

*New Hoover Quadraflex, New
Hoover Convertible, New
Hoover Dimension 900, New
Hoover Dimension 1000
Doubledecker*
1981-1986
Four vacuum cleaners, Plexiglas,
fluorescent lights
98 × 52$^1/_2$ × 27$^3/_4$ ins

*New! New Too!*
1984
Lithograph on cotton
123 × 272 ins

*New Rooomy Toyota Family
Camry*
1983
Lithograph on cotton
60 × 130 ins

*New Shelton Wet/Dry*
1981-1986
Vacuum cleaner, Plexiglas,
fluorescent lights
41 × 28 × 28 ins

*New Shelton Wet/Dry
Doubledecker*
1981
Two vacuum cleaners, Plexiglas,
fluorescent lights
82 × 28 × 28 ins

*New Shelton Wet/Dry 5-Gallon,*
*New Hoover Convertible*
*Doubledecker*
1981-1987
Two vacuum cleaners, Plexiglas,
fluorescent lights
99 × 28 × 28 ins

*New Shelton Wet/Dry 10-Gallon,*
*New Shelton Wet/Dry 5-Gallon*
*Doubledecker*
1981-1987
Two vacuum cleaners, Plexiglas,
fluorescent lights
82 × 28 × 28 ins

*New Shelton Wet/Dry*
*Tripledecker*
1981
Three vacuum cleaners, Plexiglas,
fluorescent lights
124¹/₂ × 28 × 28 ins

*New Shelton Wet/Drys 5-Gallon,*
*10-Gallon, Doubledecker*
1981-1986
Four vacuum cleaners, Plexiglas,
fluorescent lights
82 × 52 × 28 ins

*New Shop-Vac Wet/Dry*
1980
Vacuum cleaner, Plexiglas,
fluorescent lights
35 × 22 × 22 ins

*The New Jeff Koons*
1980
Duratran, lightbox
42 × 32 × 8 ins
(title page)

EQUILIBRIUM

*Aqualung*
1985
Bronze
Edition of 3 and artist's proof
27 × 17¹/₂ × 17¹/₂ ins
(illustrated p.59)

*Basketball*
1985
Bronze
Edition of 3 and artist's proof
9 ins diameter

*Boardroom*
1985
Framed 'Nike' poster
Edition of 2
31¹/₂ × 45¹/₂ ins

*Dr. Dunkenstein*
1985
Framed 'Nike' poster
Edition of 2
45¹/₂ × 31¹/₂ ins

*Dynasty on 34th Street*
1985
Framed 'Nike' poster
Edition of 2
45¹/₂ × 31¹/₂ ins

*Ice Man*
1985
Framed 'Nike' poster
Edition of 2
45 × 29¹/₂ ins

*Jam Session*
1985
Framed 'Nike' poster
Edition of 2
$31^{1}/_{2} \times 45$ ins

*Lifeboat*
1985
Bronze
Edition of 3 and artist's proof
$12 \times 80 \times 60$ ins

*Moses*
1985
Framed 'Nike' poster
Edition of 2
$45^{1}/_{2} \times 31^{1}/_{2}$ ins
(illustrated p.57)

*Mychal*
1985
Framed 'Nike' poster
Edition of 2
$45^{3}/_{4} \times 31$ ins

*One Ball 50/50 Tank*
*(Spalding Dr. J. Silver Series)*
1985
Glass, steel, distilled water,
basketball
Edition of 2
$64^{3}/_{4} \times 30^{3}/_{4} \times 13^{3}/_{4}$ ins

*One Ball Total Equilibrium Tank*
*(Spalding Dr. J. 241 Series)*
1985
Glass, steel, sodium chloride
reagent, distilled water, basketball
Edition of 2
$64^{3}/_{4} \times 30^{3}/_{4} \times 13^{3}/_{4}$ ins
(illustrated p.55)

*One Ball Total Equilibrium Tank*
*(Spalding Dr. J. Silver Series)*
1985
Glass, steel, sodium chloride
reagent, distilled water, basketball
Edition of 2
$64^{3}/_{4} \times 30^{3}/_{4} \times 13^{3}/_{4}$ ins

*Rising Stars*
1985
Framed 'Nike' poster
Edition of 2
$46 \times 32$ ins

*Secretary of Defense*
1985
Framed 'Nike' poster
Edition of 2
$45^{1}/_{2} \times 31^{1}/_{2}$ ins

*Silk*
1985
Framed 'Nike' poster
Edition of 2
$46 \times 31^{1}/_{2}$ ins

*Sir Sid*
1985
Framed 'Nike' poster
Edition of 2
$45^{3}/_{4} \times 31^{1}/_{2}$ ins

*Snorkel (Dacor)*
1985
Bronze
Edition of 3 and artist's proof
$15^{1}/_{2} \times 5 \times 1^{1}/_{4}$ ins

*Snorkel (Generic)*
1985
Bronze
Edition of 3 and artist's proof
$14^{1}/_{2} \times 5 \times 1^{1}/_{4}$ ins

*Snorkel (Shotgun)*
1985
Bronze
Edition of 3 and artist's proof
$14^{1}/_{2} \times 5 \times 2^{1}/_{2}$ ins

*Snorkel Vest*
1985
Bronze
Edition of 3 and artist's proof
$21 \times 18 \times 6$

*Soccerball (Bumblebee)*
1985
Bronze
Edition of 3 and artist's proof
$7^{1}/_{2}$ ins diameter

*Soccerball (Molten)*
1985
Bronze
Edition of 3 and artist's proof
$7^{1}/_{2}$ ins diameter

*Stormin' Norman*
1985
Framed 'Nike' poster
Edition of 2
$45 \times 31$ ins

*The Williams*
1985
Framed 'Nike' poster
Edition of 2
$45^{1}/_{2} \times 31$ ins

*Three Ball 50/50 Tank
(Dr. J. Silver Series)*
1985
Glass, steel, distilled water, three
basketballs
Edition of 2
$60^{1}/_{2} \times 48^{3}/_{4} \times 13^{1}/_{4}$ ins

*Three Ball 50/50 Tank (Two Dr.
J. Silver Series, Wilson Supershot)*
1985
Glass, steel, distilled water, three
basketballs
Edition of 2
$60^{1}/_{2} \times 48^{3}/_{4} \times 13^{1}/_{4}$ ins

*Three Ball 50/50 Tank (Wilson
Aggressor, Wilson Supershot,
Dr. J. Silver Series)*
1985
Glass, steel, distilled water, three
basketballs
Edition of 2
$60^{1}/_{2} \times 48^{3}/_{4} \times 13^{1}/_{4}$ ins
(illustrated p.61)

*Three Ball Total Equilibrium
Tank (Dr. J. Silver Series)*
1985
Glass, steel, sodium chloride
reagent, distilled water, three
basketballs
Edition of 2
$60^{1}/_{2} \times 48^{3}/_{4} \times 13^{1}/_{4}$ ins

*Three Ball Total Equilibrium
Tank (Two Dr. J. Silver Series,
Wilson Supershot)*
1985
Glass, steel, sodium chloride
reagent, distilled water, three
basketballs
Edition of 2
$60^{1}/_{2} \times 48^{3}/_{4} \times 13^{1}/_{4}$ ins

*Truck*
1985
Framed 'Nike' poster
Edition of 2
$45^{1}/_{2} \times 31^{1}/_{2}$ ins

*Two Ball 50/50 Tank*
*(Spalding Dr. J. Silver Series,*
*Spalding Dr. J.241 Series)*
1985
Glass, steel, distilled water, two
basketballs
Edition of 2
$62^3/_4 \times 36^3/_4 \times 13^1/_4$ ins

*Two Ball 50/50 Tank*
*(Spalding Dr. J. Silver Series,*
*Wilson Supershot)*
1985
Glass, steel, distilled water, two
basketballs
Edition of 2
$62^3/_4 \times 36^3/_4 \times 13^1/_4$ ins

*Two Ball Total Equilibrium Tank*
*(Spalding Dr. J. Silver Series)*
1985
Glass, steel, sodium chloride
reagent, distilled water, two
basketballs
Edition of 2
$62^3/_4 \times 36^3/_4 \times 13^1/_4$ ins

*Two Ball Total Equilibrium Tank*
*(Spalding Dr. J. Silver Series,*
*Wilson Agressor)*
1985
Glass, steel, sodium chloride
reagent, distilled water, two
basketballs
Edition of 2
$62^3/_4 \times 36^3/_4 \times 13^1/_4$ ins

*Zungul*
1985
Framed 'Nike' poster
Edition of 2
$45^3/_4 \times 31^1/_4$ ins

## LUXURY AND DEGRADATION

*Aqui Bacardi*
1986
Oil inks on canvas
Edition of 2 and artist's proof
$45 \times 60$ ins

*Baccarat Crystal Set*
1986
Stainless steel
Edition of 3 and artist's proof
$12^1/_2 \times 16 \times 16$ ins

*Come Through with Taste-Myers*
*Rum Quote Newsweek*
1986
Oil inks on canvas
Edition of 2 and artist's proof
$46 \times 60$ ins

*Find a Quiet Table*
1986
Oil inks on canvas
Edition of 2 and artist's proof
$69 \times 48$ ins

*Fisherman Golfer*
1986
Stainless steel
Edition of 3 and artist's proof
$12 \times 5 \times 8$ ins
(illustrated p.65)

*Hennessey, The Civilized Way to*
*Lay Down the Law*
1986
Oil inks on canvas
Edition of 2 and artist's proof
$45 \times 60$ ins

*I Assume You Drink Martell*
1986
Oil inks on canvas
Edition of 2 and artist's proof
45 × 60 ins

*I Could Go for Something
Gordon's*
1986
Oil inks on canvas
Edition of 2 and artist's proof
45 × 86$^1$/$_2$ ins
(illustrated p.67)

*Ice Bucket*
1986
Stainless steel
Edition of 3 and artist's proof
9$^1$/$_4$ × 7 × 12 ins

*Jim Beam – Baggage Car*
1986
Stainless steel and Bourbon
Edition of 3 and artist's proof
8$^3$/$_8$ × 16 × 6$^1$/$_2$ ins

*Jim Beam – Barrel Car*
1986
Stainless steel and Bourbon
Edition of 3 and artist's proof
7$^3$/$_4$ × 14$^1$/$_4$ × 6$^1$/$_2$ ins

*Jim Beam – Box Car*
1986
Stainless steel and Bourbon
Edition of 3 and artist's proof
7$^1$/$_2$ × 14$^1$/$_4$ × 6$^1$/$_2$ ins

*Jim Beam – Caboose*
1986
Stainless steel and Bourbon
Edition of 3 and artist's proof
8 × 14$^1$/$_4$ × 6$^1$/$_2$ ins

*Jim Beam – J.B. Turner Engine*
1986
Stainless steel and Bourbon
Edition of 3 and artist's proof
11 × 17 × 6$^1$/$_2$ ins

*Jim Beam – J.B. Turner Train*
1986
Stainless steel and Bourbon
Edition of 3 and artist's proof
11 × 114 × 6$^1$/$_2$ ins
(illustrated p.66)

*Jim Beam – Log Car*
1986
Stainless steel and Bourbon
Edition of 3 and artist's proof
7$^3$/$_4$ × 14$^1$/$_4$ × 6$^1$/$_2$ ins

*Jim Beam – Model A Ford
Pick-Up Truck*
1986
Stainless steel and Bourbon
Edition of 3 and artist's proof
6$^3$/$_4$ × 15$^1$/$_4$ × 6$^1$/$_2$ ins

*Jim Beam – Observation Car*
1986
Stainless steel and Bourbon
Edition of 3 and artist's proof
9 × 16 × 6$^1$/$_2$ ins

*Jim Beam – Passenger Car*
1986
Stainless steel and Bourbon
Edition of 3 and artist's proof
8$^3$/$_8$ × 16 × 6$^1$/$_2$ ins

*Pail*
1986
Stainless steel
Edition of 3 and artist's proof
19$^1$/$_2$ × 13 × 12$^1$/$_8$ ins

*Stay in Tonight*
1986
Oil inks on canvas
Edition of 2 and artist's proof
69 × 48 ins
(illustrated p.73)

*The Empire State of Scotch,*
*Dewars*
1986
Oil inks on canvas
Edition of 2 and artist's proof
44¹/₂ × 60 ins

*The Luxury and Degradation*
*Portfolio*
1986
Portfolio of three lithographs
Edition of 60 and 10 artist's
proofs
32 × 29 ins

*Travel Bar*
1986
Stainless steel
Edition of 3 and artist's proof
14 × 20 × 12 ins
(illustrated p.70)

STATUARY

*Bob Hope*
1986
Stainless steel
Edition of 3 and artist's proof
17 × 5¹/₂ × 5¹/₂ ins

*Cape Codder Troll*
1986
Stainless steel
Edition of 3 and artist's proof
21 × 8¹/₂ × 9 ins

*Doctor's Delight*
1986
Stainless steel
Edition of 3 and artist's proof
11 × 6³/₄ × 5³/₄ ins
(illustrated p.79)

*Flowers*
1986
Stainless steel
Edition of 3 and artist's proof
12¹/₂ × 18 × 12 ins
(illustrated p.80)

*French Coach Couple*
1986
Stainless steel
Edition of 3 and artist's proof
17 × 15¹/₂ × 11³/₄ ins

*Italian Woman*
1986
Stainless steel
Edition of 3 and artist's proof
30 × 18 × 11 ins

*Louis XIV*
1986
Stainless steel
Edition of 3 and artist's proof
46 × 27 × 15 ins
(illustrated p.77)

*Mermaid Troll*
1986
Stainless steel
Edition of 3 and artist's proof
20¹/₂ × 8¹/₂ × 8¹/₂ ins

*Rabbit*
1986
Stainless steel
Edition of 3 and artist's proof
41 × 19 × 12 ins
(illustrated p.83)

*Two Kids*
1986
Stainless steel
Edition of 3 and artist's proof
23 × 14$^1$/$_2$ × 14$^1$/$_2$ ins

KIEPENKERL

*Kiepenkerl*
1987
Stainless steel
Edition of 3 and artist's proof
71 × 26 × 37 ins
(illustrated p.87)

ART MAGAZINE ADS

*Art Magazine Ads*
1988-89
Portfolio of four colour
lithographs
Edition of 50 plus 10 artist's
proofs
45 × 37$^1$/$_4$ in
(illustrated pp.91-95)

BANALITY

*Amore*
1988
Porcelain
Edition of 3 and artist's proof
32 × 27 × 22$^1$/$_2$ ins

*Bear and Policeman*
1988
Polychromed wood
Edition of 3 and artist's proof
85 × 43 × 36 ins
(illustrated p.115)

*Buster Keaton*
1988
Polychromed wood
Edition of 3 and artist's proof
65$^3$/$_4$ × 50 × 26$^1$/$_2$ ins

*Christ and the Lamb*
1988
Gilded mirror
Edition of 3 and artist's proof
79 × 57 × 7 ins
(illustrated p.111)

*Fait d'Hiver*
1988
Porcelain
Edition of 3 and artist's proof
19$^1$/$_2$ × 63 × 31$^1$/$_2$ ins

*Little Girl*
1988
Mirror and glass
Edition of 3 and artist's proof
63 × 64$^1$/$_2$ × 3 ins

*Michael Jackson and Bubbles*
1988
Ceramic
Edition of 3 and artist's proof
42 × 70$^1$/$_2$ × 32$^1$/$_2$ ins
(illustrated p.108)

*Naked*
1988
Porcelain
Edition of 3 and artist's proof
45$^1$/$_2$ × 27 × 27 ins
(illustrated p.101)

*Pink Panther*
1988
Porcelain
Edition of 3 and artist's proof
41 × 20$^1$/$_2$ × 19 ins
(illustrated p.105)

*Popples*
1988
Porcelain
Edition of 3 and artist's proof
29$^1$/$_4$ × 23 × 12 ins
(illustrated p.99)

*St. John the Baptist*
1988
Porcelain
Edition of 3 and artist's proof
56$^1$/$_2$ × 30 × 24$^1$/$_2$ ins
(illustrated p.107)

*Serpents*
1988
Porcelain
Edition of 3 and artist's proof
23$^1$/$_2$ × 34 × 20 ins

*Stacked*
1988
Polychromed wood
Edition of 3 and artist's proof
61 × 53 × 31 ins
(illustrated p.113)

*String of Puppies*
1988
Polychromed wood
Edition of 3 and artist's proof
42 × 62 × 37 ins

*Ushering in Banality*
1988
Polychromed wood
Edition of 3 and artist's proof
38 × 62 × 30 ins
(illustrated p.102)

*Vase of Flowers*
1988
Mirror
Edition of 3 and artist's proof
72$^1$/$_2$ × 53 × 1 ins

*Winter Bears*
1988
Polychromed wood
Edition of 3 and artist's proof
48 × 44 × 15$^1$/$_2$ ins

*Wishing Well*
1988
Gilded mirror
Edition of 3 and artist's proof
87 × 56 × 8 ins

*Woman in Tub*
1988
Porcelain
Edition of 3 and artist's proof
23$^3$/$_4$ × 36 × 27 ins

*Wild Boy and Puppy*
1988
Porcelain
Edition of 3 and artist's proof
38 × 39$^1/_2$ × 23$^1/_2$ ins

*Signature Plate*
(Parkett edition plate)
1989
Porcelain with Decal
Edition of 80 and 50 artist's
proofs
10$^1/_2$ ins diameter


MADE IN HEAVEN
(Selected)

*Blow Job – Ice*
1991
Oil inks silkscreened on canvas
Unique and artist's proof
90 × 60 ins

*Blow Job (Kama Sutra)*
1991
Glass
Edition of 3 and artist's proof
23 × 18$^1/_2$ × 21$^1/_2$ ins

*Bob-Tail*
1991
Polychromed wood
Edition of 3 and artist's proof
34 × 16 × 44 ins

*Bourgeois Bust – Jeff and Ilona*
1991
Marble
Edition of 3 and artist's proof
44$^1/_2$ × 28 × 21 ins
(illustrated p.141)

*Butt Red (Close-up)*
1991
Oil inks silkscreened on canvas
Unique and artist's proof
90 × 60 ins

*Butt Red (Distance)*
1991
Oil inks silkscreened on canvas
Unique and artist's proof
90 × 60 ins

*Cat*
1991
Marble
Edition of 3 and artist's proof
18 × 14$^1/_2$ × 8$^1/_4$ ins

*Cherubs*
1991
Polychromed wood
Edition of 3 and artist's proof
48 × 43$^1/_2$ × 19 ins
(illustrated p.128)

*Couch (Kama Sutra)*
1991
Glass
Edition of 3 and artist's proof
20$^1/_2$ × 16 × 17$^3/_4$ ins

*Dirty – Ejaculation*
1991
Oil inks silkscreened on canvas
Unique and artist's proof
90 × 60 ins

*Dirty – Jeff on Top*
1991
Oil inks silkscreened on canvas
Unique and artist's proof
90 × 60 ins

*Exaltation*
1991
Oil inks silkscreened on canvas
Unique and artist's proof
90 × 60 ins

*Fingers Between Legs*
1990
Oil inks on canvas
Unique and artist's proof
96 × 144 ins

*Glass Dildo*
1991
Oil inks silkscreened on canvas
Unique and artist's proof
90 × 60 ins

*Hand on Breast*
1990
Oil inks on canvas
Unique and artist's proof
96 × 144 ins

*Head Shot*
1991
Oil inks silkscreened on canvas
Unique and artist's proof
90 × 60 ins

*Ice – Jeff on Top Pulling Out*
1991
Oil inks silkscreened on canvas
Unique and artist's proof
60 × 90 ins

*Ilona's House Ejaculation*
1991
Oil inks silkscreened on canvas
Unique and artist's proof
60 × 90 ins

*Ilona's House Ejaculation*
*(Close-up)*
1991
Oil inks silkscreened on canvas
Unique and artist's proof
60 × 90 ins

*Ilona on Top – Outdoors*
*(Kama Sutra)*
1991
Glass
Edition of 3 and artist's proof
16 × 27 × 15$^1/_2$ ins

*Ilona on Top (Rosa Background)*
1990
Oil inks on canvas
Unique and artist's proof
96 × 144 ins

*Ilona with Ass Up*
1990
Oil inks on canvas
Unique and artist's proof
96 × 144 ins

*Jeff and Ilona*
1990
Polychromed wood
Unique and artist's proof
114 × 66 × 64 ins

*Jeff Eating Ilona (Kama Sutra)*
1991
Glass
Edition of 3 and artist's proof
15$^1/_2$ × 22 × 12 ins

*Jeff in the Position of Adam*
1990
Oil inks on canvas
Unique and artist's proof
96 × 144 ins
(illustrated p.122)

*Kiss (Kama Sutra)*
1991
Glass
Edition of 3 and artist's proof
20 × 21¹/₂ × 16¹/₂ ins

*Large Vase of Flowers*
1991
Polychromed wood
Edition of 3 and artist's proof
52 × 43 × 43 ins
(illustrated p.127)

*Made in Heaven*
1989
Lithograph billboard
Edition of 3 and artist's proof
125 × 272 ins
(illustrated p.118)

*Manet*
1991
Oil inks silkscreened on canvas
Unique and artist's proof
60 × 90 ins
(illustrated p.136)

*Manet Soft*
1991
Oil inks silkscreened on canvas
Unique and artist's proof
60 × 90 ins

*Mound of Flowers*
1991
Glass
Edition of 3 and artist's proof
14 × 43 × 38 ins

*Penetration with Engagement
Ring*
1991
Oil inks silkscreened on canvas
Unique and artist's proof
60 × 90 ins

*Ponies*
1991
Oil inks silkscreened on canvas
Unique and artist's proof
90 × 60 ins

*Ponies Penetration*
1991
Oil inks silkscreened on canvas
Unique and artist's proof
90 × 60 ins

*Poodle*
1991
Polychromed wood
Edition of 3 and artist's proof
23 × 39¹/₂ × 20¹/₂ ins
(illustrated p.134)

*Position Three (Kama Sutra)*
1991
Glass
Edition of 3 and artist's proof
19 × 23³/₄ × 15⁷/₈ ins

*Red-Doggy*
1991
Oil inks silkscreened on canvas
Unique and artist's proof
60 × 90 ins

*Red Fucking*
1991
Oil inks silkscreened on canvas
Unique and artist's proof
90 × 60 ins

*Self-Portrait*
1991
Marble
Edition of 3 and artist's proof
37$^1$/$_2$ × 20$^1$/$_2$ × 14$^1$/$_2$ ins
(illustrated p.121)

*Silver Shoes*
1990
Oil inks on canvas
Unique and artist's proof
96 × 144 ins

*Three Puppies*
1991
Polychromed wood
Edition of 3 and artist's proof
19 × 27$^1$/$_4$ × 23$^1$/$_2$ ins

*Violet-Ice (Kama Sutra)*
1991
Glass
Edition of 3 and artist's proof
13 × 28 × 17 ins
(illustrated p.133)

*Wall Relief with Bird*
1991
Polychromed wood
Edition of 3 and artist's proof
72 × 50 × 27 ins
(illustrated p.139)

*White Terrier*
1991
Polychromed wood
Edition of 3 and artist's proof
20$^1$/$_2$ × 14 × 20 ins

*Wolfman (Close-up)*
1991
Oil inks silkscreened on canvas
Unique and artist's proof
90 × 60 ins
(illustrated p.131)

*Wolfman (Full-Shot)*
1991
Oil inks silkscreened on canvas
Unique and artist's proof
90 × 60 ins

*Yorkshire Terriers*
1991
Polychromed wood
Edition of 3 and artist's proof
17$^1$/$_2$ × 20$^1$/$_2$ × 17 ins
(illustrated p.124)


PUPPY

*Puppy*
1992
Live flowers, earth, wood
and steel
472 × 197 × 256 ins
(illustrated p.145)

# EXHIBITION HISTORY
# SELECTED BIBLIOGRAPHY
# FILM, TELEVISION
# AND RADIO

# JEFF KOONS

Jeff Koons was born in 1955 in York, Pennsylvania, to Henry and Gloria Koons. He studied at Maryland College of Art and the Art Institute of Chicago, and moved to New York in 1977. He lives in Munich and New York with his wife, Ilona Staller Koons.

## INDIVIDUAL EXHIBITIONS
(Selected)

1993
Anthony d'Offay Gallery, London.

1992
*Jeff Koons,* San Francisco Museum of Modern Art, and Walker Art Center, Minneapolis (July 1993).
*Jeff Koons,* Stedelijk Museum, Amsterdam, and Staatsgalerie Stuttgart (March 1993).
*Made in Heaven*, Galerie Lehmann, Lausanne.

1991
*Made in Heaven*, Galerie Max Hetzler, Cologne.
*Made in Heaven*, Sonnabend Gallery, New York.

1989
*Jeff Koons-Nieuw Werk*, Galerie 'T Venster, Rotterdam.

1988
*Jeff Koons*, Museum of Contemporary Art, Chicago.
*Banality*, Sonnabend Gallery, New York.
*Banality*, Galerie Max Hetzler, Cologne.
*Banality*, Donald Young Gallery, Chicago.

1987
*The New: Encased Works 1981-1986*, Daniel Weinberg Gallery, Los Angeles.

1986
*Luxury and Degradation*, International with Monument Gallery, New York.
*Luxury and Degradation*, Daniel Weinberg Gallery, Los Angeles.

1985
*Equilibrium*, International with Monument Gallery, New York.
*Equilibrium*, Feature Gallery, Chicago.

1980
*The New,* The New Museum of Contemporary Art, New York.

## GROUP EXHIBITIONS
(Selected)

1992
*Strange Developments*, Anthony d'Offay Gallery, London.
*Made for Arolsen*, Schloss Arolsen, Germany.
*Double Take*, Hayward Gallery, London.

1991
*Objects for the Ideal Home*,
  Serpentine Gallery, London.
*Metropolis*, Martin-Gropius Bäu,
  Berlin.

1990
*High & Low: Modern Art and
  Popular Culture*, The Museum of
  Modern Art, New York, The Art
  Institute of Chicago, and The
  Museum of Contemporary Art,
  Los Angeles.
*Artificial Nature*, Deste Foundation
  for Contemporary Art, Athens.
*Aperto*, Venice Biennale, Venice.
*The 8th Biennale of Sydney*,
  Sydney Beach.
*1990 - Energies*, Stedelijk
  Museum, Amsterdam.
*New Work: A New Generation*,
  San Francisco Art Museum,
  San Francisco.
*Horn of Plenty*, Stedelijk
  Museum, Amsterdam.
*Culture and Commentary*,
  Hirshhorn Museum and
  Sculpture Garden, Smithsonian
  Institute, Washington, D.C.

1989
*Image World*, Whitney Museum
  of American Art, New York.
*Mit Dem Fernrohr Durch Die*,
  Kunstgeschichte, Kunsthalle Basel.
*A Forest of Signs: Art in the Crisis
  of Representation*, Museum of
  Contemporary Art, Los Angeles.
*Whitney Biennial*, Whitney
  Museum of American Art,
  New York.

*Suburban Home Life: Tracking
  the American Dream*, Whitney
  Museum of American Art at
  Federal Plaza, New York.

1988
*The Carnegie International*,
  The Carnegie Museum of Art,
  Pittsburgh.
*L'Object de L'Exposition*, Centre
  National des Arts Plastiques,
  Paris.
*Collection Pour Une Region*,
  CAPC Musée d'Art
  Contemporain de Bordeaux.
*New York Art Now: Part Two*,
  Saatchi Collection, London.
*Art at the End of the Social*,
  Rooseum Gasverksgaten, Malmo.
*The Bi-National*, Institute of
  Contemporary Arts, Boston, and
  Kunsthalle, Dusseldorf.

1987
*Collection Sonnabend*, Centro de
  Arte Reina Sofia, Madrid, and
  CAPC Musée d'Art
  Contemporain de Bordeaux.
*NY Art Now*, Saatchi Collection,
  London.
*Avant-Garde in the Eighties*, Los
  Angeles County Museum of Art.
*Les Courtiers du Desir*, Galeries
  Contemporaines, Centre Georges
  Pompidou, Paris.
*Whitney Biennial*, Whitney
  Museum of American Art,
  New York.
*Skulptur Projekte*, Münster.

1986

*Art and Its Double*, Barcelona and Madrid.

*Endgame: Reference and Simulation in Recent Painting and Sculpture*, Institute of Contemporary Art, Boston.

*New Sculpture*, Renaissance Society, University of Chicago.

*Damaged Goods*, The New Museum of Contemporary Art, New York.

Sonnabend Gallery, New York.

1985

*Affiliations: Recent Sculpture and Its Antecedents*, Whitney Museum of American Art, Stanford.

*Objects in Collision*, The Kitchen, New York.

1984

*A Decade of New Art*, Artist's Space, New York.

1983

*Los Angeles - New York Exchange*, Artist's Space, New York, and LACE, Los Angeles.

*Objects, Structures and Artifices*, University of South Florida, Tampa, and Bucknell University, Lewisburg.

1982

*A Fatal Attraction: Art and the Media*, Renaissance Society, University of Chicago.

*Energie New York*, Espace Lyonnais d'Art Contemporain.

1981

*Lighting*, P.S.1, Long Island City, New York.

BIBLIOGRAPHY
(Selected)

*Catalogues*

John Caldwell et. al., *Jeff Koons*, San Francisco Museum of Modern Art (December 1992).

Viet Lohrs, *Made for Arolsen*, Schloss Arolsen (12 June 1992).

Matthew Collings, 'Jeff Koons', *Pop Art*, Royal Academy of Art, London (January 1992), pp.38-47.

Marco Livingstone, 'The Legacy of Pop Art', *Objects for the Ideal Home*, Serpentine Gallery, London (September 1991), p.1.

Eds., 'Jeff Koons', *Metropolis*, Martin-Gropius-Bau, Berlin (20 April 1991), pp.174-6.

Kirk Varnedoe and Adam Gopnik, 'Contemporary Reflections', *High and Low*, Museum of Modern Art, New York (7 October 1990), pp.368-403.

K.M., 'Jeff Koons', *Pharmakon'90* (28 July 1990), pp.240-9 and Jeff Koons, 'Jeff Koons', *Pharmakon'90*, Tokyo (28 July 1990), pp.45-7.

René Block, 'The Readymade Boomerang', *Art is Easy*, Sydney Biennial (7 April 1990), pp.18,19,422-42.

Curators, 'Jeff Koons', *Whitney Biennial*, Whitney Museum of American Art, New York (26 April 1989), pp.72-5.

Jeff Koons and Martin Kippenberger, 'Collaborations', *Parkett* (No.19, 1989).

Michael Danoff, *Jeff Koons*, Art Institute of Chicago (July 1988).

Dan Cameron, 'Introduction', *NY Art Now*, Saatchi Collection, London (January 1988), pp.125-39.

Germano Celant, 'The Marble Period', *Unexpressionism* (January 1988), pp.5-29.

Eugene Schwartz, 'Post Abstract Abstraction', *Post Abstract Abstraction*, Aldrich Museum of Contemporary Art, Ridgefield, Connecticut (31 May 1987), p.41.

R. Armstrong, L. Phillips and R. Marshall, 'Introduction', *Whitney Biennial*, Whitney Museum of American Art, New York (10 April 1987).

Dan Cameron, 'Art and its Double', *Art and its Double* (27 November 1986), pp.68-73.

Hal Foster, 'The Future Illusion', *Endgame*, Institute of Contemporary Art, Boston (25 September 1986), pp.91-107.


*Periodicals and Newspapers*

Jutta Koether, 'Puppy Logic', *Artforum* (September 1992), p.90.

Christian Kammerling, 'Jeff Koons', *Suddeutsche Zeitung Magazin* (November 1992).

Peter Schjeldahl, 'The Documenta of the Dog', *Art in America* (September 1992), pp.88-97.

Roberta Smith, 'How Much Is That Doggy', *New York Times* (5 July 1992), p.27.

Sibylle Fritsch, 'Putten, Puppies, Pornos', *Profil* (9 June 1992), pp.72-6.

Eds., 'U2', *Stern* (21 May 1992) pp.128-39.

Adam Gopnik, 'Lust For Life', *New Yorker* (18 May 1992), pp.76-8.

Hildegund Amanshauser, 'Pornographic Scenes of A Normal Married Life', *Kamera Austria* (May 1992), pp.35-45.

Annie Sprinkle, 'Hard Core Heaven', *Arts* (March 1992), pp.46-8.

Renato Barilli, 'Jeff Koons', *L'Uomo Vogue* (March 1992), pp.128-33.

Sylvere Lotringer, 'Immaculate Conceptualism', *Artscribe* (January/February 1992), pp.24-5.

Carter Ratcliff, 'Not For Repro', *Artforum* (January/February 1992), pp.82-7.

Daniel Pinchbeck, 'Kitsch and Rich', *The Sunday Times Magazine* (12 January 1992) pp.28-34.

Judd Tully, 'Jeff Koons Raw Talent', *The Washington Post* (15 December 1991), p.1.

Anthony Haden-Guest, 'Art or Commerce?' *Vanity Fair* (November 1991), pp.200-5, 254.

Jeff Koons, 'Why is David Lynch Important?', *Parkett* (No.28, 1991), p.156.

Jeffrey Deitch, 'L'Industria Dell'Arte', *Flash Art* (May/June 1991), pp.72-5.

Rob Malasch, 'Adam en Eva', *Parool* (31 May 1991), p.1.

Linda van Nunen, 'Loony Koons', *Studio* (February 1991), pp.88-9, 170.

Donald Kuspit, 'Sincere Cynicism', *Arts* (December 1990), pp.60-5.

Roberta Smith, 'High and Low Culture', *New York Times* (5 October 1990), pp.C1, C25.

Robert Storr, 'Jeff Koons: Gym Dandy', *Art Press* (October 1990), pp.14-23.

Andrew Renton, 'Jeff Koons and the Art of the Deal: Marketing (as) Sculpture', *Performance* (September 1990), pp.18-29.

Dodie Kazanjian, 'Koons Crazy', *Vogue* (August 1990), pp.338-43.

Andrew Renton, 'Jeff Koons: I have my finger on the eternal', *Flash Art* (May/June 1990), pp.110-5.

Peter Schjeldahl, 'Jeff Koons', *Objectives* (8 May 1990), pp.82-99.

Andrew Renton, 'Jeff Koons', *Flash Art* (May/June 1990), pp.108-14.

Sarah Morris and Remo Guidieri, 'Jeff Koons', *Galeries Magazine* (March/April 1990), pp.126-33.

Eds., 'Jeff Koons', *German Elle* (April 1990), p.98.

Peter Schjeldahl, 'In your Eye', *7 Days* (10 October 1990), pp.70-1.

Andrew Renton, 'Super Star', *Blitz* (January 1990), pp.52-9.

James Hall, 'Neo-Geo's Bachelor Artists', *Art International* (December 1989), pp.30-45.

Lisa Philips, 'Art and Media Culture', *Image World* (18 November 1989), pp.57-70, 125.

Peter Schjeldahl, 'Jeff Koons', *7 Days* (12 July 1989), p.14.

Michael Compton, 'Jeff Koons & Co.' *Art & Design* (8 July 1989), pp.38-45.

Jeff Koons, 'Jeff Koons', *Artforum* (May/June 1989), p.134.

Matthew Collings, 'You are a White Man', *Modern Painters* (June 1989), pp.60-3.

Dan Cameron, 'Art and Its Double', *Flash Art* (May/June 1989), pp.58-71.

Daniel Pinchbeck, 'Jeff Koons', *Splash* (April 1989).

Stuart Morgan, 'Jeff Koon's Fun', *Artscribe* (March/April 1989), pp.46-9.

Jeff Koons, 'Exploitation', *Defunct!* (February 1989), p.4.

Hilton Kramer, 'Koons Show', *New York Observer* (19 December 1988), pp.1,11.

Peter Schjeldahl, 'Loony Koons', *7 Days* (14 December 1988), pp.66-7.

Isabell Graw, 'Carnegie International', *Galleries* (December 1988) pp.76-8.

Alan Jones, 'Thriller', *Contemporanea* (September 1988), pp.42-5.

Peter Plagens, 'The Emporor's New Cherokee', *Art in America* (June 1988), pp.23-4.

Paul Taylor, 'Cultural Geometry', *Flash Art* (May/June 1988), pp.124-45.

Klaus Ottman, 'Jeff Koons', *Journal of Contemporary Art* (May 1988), pp.18-23.

Roberta Smith, 'Rituals of Consumption', *Art in America* (May 1988), pp.164-70.

Veit Loers, 'Interview with Jeff Koons', *Schlaf der Vernuft* (21 Febuary 1988).

Jerry Saltz, 'The Dark Side of the Rabbit', *Arts* (February 1988), pp.26-7.

Jeffery Deitch, 'Cultural Geometry', *Flash Art* (January/February 1988), p.21.

Jeff Koons, 'A Project For Artforum', *Artforum* (November/December 1987).

Andrew Graham-Dixon, 'Neo-Geo', *Vogue* (June 1987), pp.360-6.

Lynne Cooke, 'Object Lessons', *Artscribe* (September/October 1987) pp.55-9.

Eleanor Heartney, 'Sighted in Munster', *Art in America* (September 1987), pp.140-3, 201.

Michael Benson, 'Art: The Munster Sculpture Project', *New York Times*, (22 June 1987) p.C13.

Dan Cameron, 'Art and its Double Life', *Flash Art* (May/June 1987), pp.57-71.

Giancarlo Politi, 'Interview', *Flash Art* (January/February 1987), pp.71-6.

Shaun Calry, 'Review', *Flash Art* (January/February 1987), p.104.

Anthony Haden-Guest, 'Art of Musical Chairs', *Vanity Fair* (January 1987), pp.60-8.

Ronald Jones, 'Jeff Koons at International', *Artscribe* (January/February 1986), pp.72-3.

Daniela Salvioni, 'McCollum and Koons', *Flash Art* (November/December 1986), pp.66-8.

Peter Schjeldahl, 'Salon of Autumn 1986', *Art in America* (December 1986), pp.15-21.

Roberta Smith, 'Art: Four Young East Villagers, *New York Times* (24 October 1986), pp.C30.

Kim Levin, 'His Best Shot', *Village Voice* (14 October 1986), p.96.

Ronald Jones, 'Damaged Goods', *Flash Art* (October 1986), p.73-4.

Jeffrey Deitch, 'A New Dawn', *Modern Objects* (2 August 1986) pp.1-6.

Matthew Collings, 'Mythologies', *Artscribe* (March/April 1986), pp.22-6.

Gary Indiana, 'Jeff Koons', *Art in America* (November 1985), pp.162-4.

## FILM, TELEVISION AND RADIO

### 1992

*Jeff Koons*, South Bank Show, LWT, London.
*Tonight with Jonathan Ross*, Channel 4 TV, London.
*The Word*, Channel 4 TV, London.
*Even Better Than The Real Thing*, U2, MTV.
*Schlusselloch*, Germany.
*Fashion Television*, VH1, May 21.
*Fox Style News:* Fox TV, April 16.
*Dennis Miller Show*, Fox TV, April 1.
*Real Sex 3*, HBO, February 28.
*The Edge*, PBS, January 15.

### 1991

*The Late Show*, BBC TV, London.
*Is it Art or Smut?*, Geraldo, Network, December 4.
*This Morning*, CBS TV (live), New York.
*Inside Bunte*, German TV.
*VSIA*, Helskini TV.
*The Art Merry-Go-Round*, Marijke Jongbloed, Netherlands.
*Art in the Age of Mass Culture*, M. Blackwood Productions, Inc.
*Modern Art in the Age of Disney*, P. von Brandenberg, New York.
*Jeff Koons*, Ari Marcopoulos, New York.
*Ein Amerikanisches Schicksal: Der Kunstler Jeff Koons*, Heinz Peter Schwerfel, Germany.

### 1990

*Tonight with Jonathan Ross*, Channel 4 TV, London.
*Jeff Koons* (Swatch), MTV Europe.
*New York Special*, RTL 4, Netherlands.
*My Name is Andy Warhol*, Leo Scheer, France.
*The World of Art: Artists in Profile*, CNN, New York.
*Kulturen*, Sveriges TV, Sweden.
*La Biennale Di Venezia*, Studio Mestiere Cinema, Venice.
*Jeff Koons: The Banality Show*, ART/New York (#31).
*Kaleidoscope*, BBC Radio 4, London.

### 1989

*The Late Show*, BBC Television, London.
*Andy Warhol*, The Eleventh Hour (#134), London.
*American Art Today: 1989 Biennial Exhibition*, Whitney Museum of Art, New York.

### 1988

*Jeff Koons*, Museum of Contemporary Art, Chicago.

## NOTES

All statements by Jeff Koons are extracted from published interviews or are published for the first time.

Sources for 'Phrases and Philosophies' in order of appearance: *The Edge*, Channel 13/PBS, 1991. Andrew Renton, 'Jeff Koons: I have my finger on the eternal', *Flash Art* (May/June 1990), pp.110-15. Jeff Koons, 1992. Dan Cameron, 'Art and its Double Life', *Flash Art* (May/June 1987), pp.57-71. Andrew Renton, 'Jeff Koons and the Art of the Deal: Marketing (as) Sculpture', *Performance* (September 1990), pp.18-29. Louise Baring, 'The Man Who Sold Michael Jackson', *The Mail on Sunday* (18 March 1990), pp.1-3. Koons, 1991. *Flash Art*, 1987. Koons, 1990. Koons, 1991. *Flash Art*, 1987. Daniel Pinchbeck, 'Jeff Koons', *Splash* (April 1989). Koons, 1992. Dennis Barricklow, 'Jeff Koons', *The Face* (27 November 1990), pp.104-8. Koons, 1992. Eds., 'Jeff Koons', *German Elle* (April 1990), p.98. Roger Tredre, 'La Cicciolina and her "amore" gives drinkers a kitsch performance', *The Independent* (22 February 1992). Dodie Kazanjian, 'Koons Crazy', *Vogue* (August 1990), pp.338-43. *Flash Art*, 1990. *Flash Art*, 1987. Burke & Hare, 'From Full Fathom Five', *Parkett* (No.19, 1989), p.45. *Flash Art*, 1987. Koons, 1992. Panel discussion: Jeff Koons, 1991 Hoffman Distinguished Lecturer, Dallas Museum of Modern Art, Dallas, Texas (5 December 1991). Howard Jacobson, 'The Bride Stripped Bare by her Husband Already', *Modern Painters* (Winter 1991), pp.30-3. *The Edge*, 1991. Koons, 1992. *Flash Art*, 1987.

Sources for statements opposite plates are given by page reference. Koons, 1992: pp.42, 44, 58, 60, 78, 86, 104, 126, 138, 144. *Flash Art*, 1987: pp.48, 54, 64, 72. Interview with Stefan Hildebrandt, Cologne (14 December 1991): p.50. *Vogue*, 1990: pp.56,82, 106, 114, 120, 130, 140. Dallas Museum of Modern Art, 1991: p.76. *Splash*, 1989: pp.90, 92, 100, 110, 112. Anthony Haden-Guest, 'Art or Commerce?', *Vanity Fair* (November 1991), pp.200-5, 254: p.98.

## PHOTOGRAPHIC CREDITS

Kevin Clarke, p.59; Greg Crawford, pp.45-51; Klaus Frahm, back cover; Greg Gorman, pp.91-5; Jeff Koons, p.43; Douglas M. Parker, pp.65-73; San Francisco Museum of Modern Art, p.109; Fred Scruton, pp.77-87; Riccardo Schicchi, pp.119, 123, 131, 137; Dieter Schwerdtle, p.145; Jim Strong, pp.99-115, 121, 125-9, 133-5, 129-41; Zindman/Fremont, pp.55, 61.

## ACKNOWLEDGMENTS

The publisher and the Anthony d'Offay Gallery would like to thank
Jeff Koons for his collaboration on this book, and Robert Rosenblum for
his introduction. We are also indebted to Sarah Morris and
Gary McCraw of Jeff Koons Inc. Productions for their invaluable help,
and to Ilona Staller Koons, Jeffrey Deitch, Max Hetzler, Uwe Kraus,
Herman Lelie, Knut Wilhelm, Tim Egan, Dave Etheridge,
and Irena Hoare.

First published in 1992 in the United States of America by
Rizzoli International Publications, Inc., 300 Park Avenue South,
New York, NY 10010

ISBN 0–8478–1696–6
LC: 92–56762

With Jeff Koons
Coordinated by Robert Violette
Edited by Sadie Coles and Robert Violette
Designed by Herman Lelie
Typeset by Goodfellow & Egan, Cambridge
Produced in Germany by Uwe Kraus Gmbh, Murr
Printed in Germany

Frontispiece: *The New Jeff Koons,* 1980.